NAVIGATING THE NEWBORN STAGE

A Practical and Spiritual Guide to the First Four Weeks

Amy Joy Fox

Copyright © 2017 Amy Joy Fox.

All rights reserved. No part of this book may be used or reproduced by any means, graphic, electronic, or mechanical, including photocopying, recording, taping or by any information storage retrieval system without the written permission of the author except in the case of brief quotations embodied in critical articles and reviews.

This book is a work of non-fiction. Unless otherwise noted, the author and the publisher make no explicit guarantees as to the accuracy of the information contained in this book and in some cases, names of people and places have been altered to protect their privacy.

WestBow Press books may be ordered through booksellers or by contacting:

WestBow Press
A Division of Thomas Nelson & Zondervan
1663 Liberty Drive
Bloomington, IN 47403
www.westbowpress.com
1 (866) 928-1240

Because of the dynamic nature of the Internet, any web addresses or links contained in this book may have changed since publication and may no longer be valid. The views expressed in this work are solely those of the author and do not necessarily reflect the views of the publisher, and the publisher hereby disclaims any responsibility for them.

Any people depicted in stock imagery provided by Thinkstock are models, and such images are being used for illustrative purposes only. Certain stock imagery © Thinkstock.

Scripture quotations are from the ESV® Bible (The Holy Bible, English Standard Version®), copyright © 2001 by Crossway, a publishing ministry of Good News Publishers. Used by permission. All rights reserved.

Scripture quotations taken from the New American Standard Bible® (NASB), Copyright © 1960, 1962, 1963, 1968, 1971, 1972, 1973, 1975, 1977, 1995 by The Lockman Foundation Used by permission. www.Lockman.org

ISBN: 978-1-5127-9978-1 (sc)
ISBN: 978-1-5127-9977-4 (hc)
ISBN: 978-1-5127-9979-8 (e)

Library of Congress Control Number: 2017912399

Print information available on the last page.

WestBow Press rev. date: 8/24/2017

CONTENTS

Preface vii

Section 1

A Four-Week Study 1

Section 2

Chapter 1   Taking a Spiritual Inventory 61
Chapter 2   Life Has a Way of Changing 67
Chapter 3   Managing Your Emotions 75
Chapter 4   Healing From Your Birth 79
Chapter 5   How Hubby Fits In 83
Chapter 6   Baby Basics: Sleeping & Eating 89
Chapter 7   Long-Term Spiritual Fruitfulness 95
Appendix A Healing from a Traumatic Birth 97
Notes 105

PREFACE

> Making the decision to have a child is momentous.
> It is to decide forever to have your heart go walking
> around outside your body. – By Elizabeth Stone[1]

I love that quote by Elizabeth Stone. It is definitely true. Having a baby is such a joy, and it is like taking a piece of your heart and putting it into another person. Our love for our babies makes it possible for us to sacrifice our time, sleep, and sanity for our kids. They tend to want to steal our hearts, and we are willing to give it. That doesn't mean being a mom is easy. The journey of motherhood might be tough, but it is all worth it in the end.

If you are still pregnant, you are growing a human being inside your body! There is something to be said about the wonder of how God created a woman's body. The ability to grow a baby, deliver it and then feed it once it arrives is a wonder. Just realize you will soon have one of God's miracles in your arms. I know it seems like a lot of pressure, but it is still awesome to think about.

If you have already had your miracle, consider how crazy it is that not only did your body just make a baby; it also made its way out of you. You really should be so proud of yourself no matter how labor went. If it didn't go as planned and you feel disappointed about it, give yourself time to heal and process the whole experience. I had more than a few people tell me how they went into the hospital with what felt like period cramps and a few hours later they popped out a baby. Don't feel guilty if that wasn't you. We all have our own unique story.

Now, you may be wondering why I decided to write a study book for the first few weeks postpartum. Let's just say that I've always enjoyed studying and praying. They've been a priority in my life for quite a while, and then suddenly after the birth of my daughter I got off track, I was shocked, to say the least. It was maybe three weeks into my postpartum life when I started to study again, and by that I mean, trying to read a little of my Bible while my mind was asleep from night feedings. I found, though, that after I started to study again that I began coping with the changes in my life much better. The Lord filled me up with His strength while I battled sleep depravity and being overwhelmed. Well, four months later I found out I was pregnant again! (My kids are one year and three weeks apart). As time came close to give birth the second time, I started to search for a study book to keep me on track in my walk with the Lord. I needed something that was short, sweet and to the point. I found a few, but nothing that was related to pregnancy or what I was going to go through. It honestly made me a little frustrated, and that is where the idea to write a book started. I felt God had laid it on my heart by showing me a tremendous need, mainly my own need, to have a study book for the first few weeks after delivery. In August of 2016, I gave birth to a big (10lb 4oz) baby boy. Shortly after having my son, I started writing down verses about the different struggles I was facing being a mom of a newborn. Out of that the study guide you are about to use was born.

A lot goes on in the first four weeks after delivery, which you will soon find out. You are learning how to take care of your newborn and all that goes along with that. My mom was so worried about me since I was trying to write a book during that crazy time, but I believe God was calling me to write it, so I did it anyway. The first few weeks are very intense, and that is why the study guide was written while I was going through them, so I could relate to what you are going through right now. I pray that as you start this journey of motherhood, God will guide you through it as you learn to love, to heal and continue to put Him first.

Amy Fox

SECTION 1

A FOUR-WEEK STUDY

Congratulations on becoming a mom! I'd like to be the first to welcome you to your "new mom" study guide. As a new mom, when it comes to studying you must go back to the basics. You don't have time for all the extras right at the beginning so going back to the basics is very important. You need to get the most "bang for your buck" regarding study time. You will have less time to study than before and more distractions, really only one very adorable distraction. Wayne Mack has some good and simple goals for your study time.

- "Worship: to get to know Him, to be humbled by His Holiness, comforted by His love, strengthened by His presence."
- "Change: to root out sins and establish biblical attitudes and actions in your life."[2]

    Being pregnant or having a baby can seem like an excuse for dropping your study but it doesn't have to be. God has brought you into this situation and desires to teach you through it. As I experienced, you will need God even more in this time to correctly process and deal with what you are going through both physically and emotionally. After the birth of my first child, I remember about a week after I had her I was miserable and overwhelmed. My husband, being the spiritual leader I needed, looked at me when I was crying and complaining about how tired I was asked, "When was the last time you studied or prayed?" It was like a smack in the face. I had been consistently studying for well over ten years, and the birth of a baby made me completely lose track of it. How dare he ask me such a question, especially while I was suffering? It was a wake-up call and helped me see the importance of getting back my time with the Lord. Elizabeth George wrote in her book, *Loving God With All Your Mind*, that as mothers, we seem to be constantly needed. Only after studying and having time with God can we "give to others because we will have already received from the Father the guidance, perspective, strength, and grace we need for the day."[3] In the first few weeks, your baby will need everything from you, and that can be tough especially if you aren't being filled up yourself. Hopefully, these verses you are about to study will give you the encouragement to keep going and will fill up what is lacking in your soul.

With these ideas in mind, press forward in making the most of the little time you have to focus on the Lord. Only then will you find peace, comfort and the strength to move forward.

DAY 1

"For you formed my inward parts; you wove me in my mother's womb. I will give thanks to You, for I am fearfully and wonderfully made; Wonderful are your works, and my soul knows it very well. My frame was not hidden from You, when I was being made in secret, and skillfully wrought in the depths of the earth; Your eyes have seen my unformed substance; and in Your book were all written the days that were ordained for me, when as yet there was not of them."
Psalm 139: 13–16

Congratulations again on the birth of your baby! God has spent the last nine months or so being intricately involved in creating every detail of your new baby. God's hand in the creation of your son or daughter is truly amazing. We take great comfort knowing God formed your baby because not all children come out in good health or right on time. I know when my daughter arrived she had a heart defect and her kidney was in the wrong spot. This was really hard for me to deal with. But what a comfort to know that God had that all planned out. He made her like she is for a reason and it was not a mistake. God has made your son or daughter just the way He wanted to. He has ordained a special plan for their life.

What part of the verse really sticks out to you? _____
_____
If you are struggling, how is this verse a comfort to you?
_____
_____

DAY 2

"Just as you do not know the path of the wind and how bones are formed in the womb of the pregnant woman, so you do not know the activity of God who makes all things."
Ecclesiastes 11:5

Read the verse again and just think about it for a minute. Think about how a baby is formed, has there been a doctor who can fully explain the phenomenon of a baby growing inside of you? How can bones form out of cells? How about hair color, eye color, personality, fingers, toes or their cute little cheeks? This is definitely a current-day miracle!!

You got to witness first hand a miracle of God, how does that make you feel about the experience? _____
_____

How should you respond to seeing such a miracle? _____
_____

DAY 3

> "To the woman He said, 'I will greatly multiply your pain in childbirth, In pain you will bring forth children'"
> Genesis 3:16a

My wise mother brought this verse to my attention after the birth of my son. I was struggling with how terrible, demeaning and painful my birth was. I thought that nothing could have topped how hard my labor with my daughter was and yet this had exceeded it. I had talked to other women who had very easy and pain–free births. How could this happen to me? Why did my body seem to refuse to go into natural labor? I thought birth was supposed to be a natural and wonderful process and mine required an induction every time. As I was dealing with the emotions of this my mom said, "Amy, you keep forgetting that labor is cursed." I had never thought of it that way. In that moment, God enlightened me and I saw my whole birth in a different perspective. I had failed to apply God's word to my situation. I was comparing my labor with my own ideas and coming up short. This led to feelings of inadequacy and failure on my part that God wasn't asking me to bear.

What are some things you wish you could have changed about your birth experience? _____
_____

DAY 4

*"You will keep him in perfect peace, whose mind
is stayed on You because he trusts in You."*
Isaiah 26:3 (NASB)

At times, I am sure you wish for a moment of peace and quiet, but this is not talking exactly about that kind of peace. It is more of an inner calm that brings you through the difficult times. I know you have probably been waking up every 2 ½ to 3 hours and spending every waking hour learning to take care of your precious baby. Maybe, you are fighting with your husband, or you feel overwhelmed. Your hormones are trying to get back to normal, and that is causing a large range of emotions. The roller coaster of emotions is crazy, and you may be wondering where the "peace of God" is. How or more importantly where do you get it? Isaiah 26:3 gives us the secret. It is a mind stayed on God. A mind that trusts in Him has this kind of peace. God needs to be your anchor, and that is why your time with God is so important. You need to keep focused on Him to help anchor your raging emotions. God knows what you are going through, the emotions and the ups and downs even if no one else does. God promises you peace if you just focus on Him. It is gained through study, praying and dwelling on His word. Though it is hard, you will need to believe God to bring you through.

How can you keep your mind "stayed" on God? Some examples could be listening to Christian music or sermons online, just to get you started. _____
_____

DAY 5

> "Cast your burden upon the Lord and He will sustain you;"
> Psalm 55:22a

Cast your burden upon the Lord and He will sustain you… The two words that stick out to me are "burden" and "sustain." There is nothing like motherhood that brings those two words closer together. Do you have a burden? Of course, you do as you try and figure out how to take care your little one. Along with that, taking care of yourself and the emotions you are dealing with definitely constitutes as a burden. "The word for 'burden' implies one's circumstances, one's lot."[4] Burden does not necessarily have to be negative, just difficult. Having a baby to take care of is a wonderful thing, those beautiful eyes, the little toes, and fingers. Your baby needs you to be able to survive or in this case be "sustained." It is a lot of work to take care of a newborn; they need a lot out of you, your time, your tender care, your help, and love. I would call this a positive burden. You will need to be filled up with love, patience, and peace to give to them what they need, and God must be your source. He will sustain you, but you need to go to Him with your burdens in prayer. He promises to help you just ask.

Have you asked God for His sustaining power? You can do that by casting your burdens on Him. _____

DAY 6

> "I would have despaired unless I had believed that I would see the goodness of the Lord in the land of the living.
> Wait for the Lord; Be strong and let your heart take courage;
> Yes, wait for the Lord."
> Psalm 27:13–14

I like the NASB version of this verse where it adds, "I would have despaired…" There are moments you will experience despair, whether it is from the vast array of emotions you are feeling or if you are suffering from postpartum depression. God has the answers to solving both of these issues. Motherhood is not for the faint-hearted, and everyone has these moments of despair. You will feel like you can't keep going, you are too tired and worn out. You keep fighting with your husband or the pain from birth is too much to deal with. God gives you the cure for these times of despair. First, believe and trust you will see God's goodness again; even if you don't feel like it. Remind yourself "this too shall pass." Second, wait on God. Pray to Him, ask Him for help and wait for Him to answer. Third, be strong and take courage. This is the same thing that God said countless times to Joshua when he was taking over Moses' spot. You must be confident that God won't forsake you. Only then will you gain the strength and confidence you need to wait patiently for God's help and not to despair. You may not be able to see the goodness of God in your situation right now, but it is there. Wait and search for it.

What are some good things that God has done for you lately or in the past? _____

_____

DAY 7

> "The steadfast love of the Lord never ceases; His mercies never come to an end they are new every morning; great is your faithfulness."
> Lamentations 3:22–23 (NIV)

It's 11:50 pm and the baby has been crying for hours. You are frazzled and tired; you just want to go to bed; it has been another long day, and nothing will soothe your little one. These are the moments you need to cry out to God even more than normal. You may feel empty of love and don't think you can move on. I believe He gave you this verse in Lamentations. When the Israelites were in exile this verse was to comfort them and remind them that God's love and His mercies were never coming to an end. The best part is that "they are NEW every morning." I remember in those moments, late at night I would repeat this verse and say, "I only have ten minutes until morning, Lord I am ready for your new dose of mercy and love." Knowing that at twelve am it would be the morning and that He was faithful to give me a fresh dose of mercy and love made me able to last a few more minutes. It calmed my frazzled nerves so I could calm my baby.

Recount one time that God has been faithful to you. _____
_____

Ask Him for His steadfast love and mercies.

DAY 8

> "You have taken account of my wanderings;
> Put my tears in Your bottle.
> Are they not in Your book?"
> Psalm 56:8

King David wrote this Psalm when he was in the process of running from Saul. He was in hiding and afraid for his life. Though you are not running for your life, you can still see a glimpse of God's comfort. He knew God had "taken account" of where he was going and his wanderings. He was under deep emotional stress and had been crying over his circumstances. Sound a lot like you feel? Don't worry, the Comforter puts your tears in His bottle and writes them in His book. God takes account of your circumstances: your hard labor, your difficulty breastfeeding or bottle-feeding, your tears over your pain and your emotions. He ordained this situation, and He causes a womb to become pregnant. He walks with you the entire way. Cry out to Him. Ask Him for help. He hears you and keeps track of the things that make you cry. You might feel He is the only one who understands you and He does. So talk to Him about what you are dealing with and let His comfort surround you.

What are a few things you have been crying over today? _____
_____

Spend a moment talking to God about it.

DAY 9

"Brethren, I do not regard myself as having laid hold of it yet;. But one thing I do: forgetting what lies behind and reaching forward to what lies ahead, I press on toward the goal for the prize of the upward call of God in Christ Jesus."
Philippians 3:13–14

I happened to be studying "Loving God With All Your Mind" by Elizabeth George, after the birth of baby number two. This verse was paramount for me moving on from my traumatic birth (See Appendix A). God calls you and me to move forward, to press on. It is so easy to get stuck emotionally or mentally. No matter what kind of birth you had, you must continue to move forward in your walk with the Lord. The first step is to "forget what lies behind." Don't let what has happened trip you up. You need to deal with your emotions about your labor and the frustration that you may be feeling over your life changing. Being a new mom is hard. You might feel trapped at home or feel you no longer have a life apart from the baby. This can trap you spiritually. You might wonder or ask why God has put you here and get mad at Him for it. You may wish for other things, maybe to go back to work or maybe the opportunity to be a stay-at-home mom. You must deal with the fact that God has put you here and ordained this circumstance. Accept that this is God's plan for your life right now and figure out your new routine. If you are constantly looking back, you will not forget what was behind: your job, your so-called freedom to come and go as you please, your wants, a life without kids. Don't get stuck in the past, "forget what lies behind."

What is something in your past that is holding you back from moving forward? _____

_____

DAY 10

> "Brethren, I do not regard myself as having laid hold of it yet; But one thing I do: forgetting what lies behind and reaching forward to what lies ahead, I press on toward the goal for the prize of the upward call of God in Christ Jesus."
> Philippians 3:13–14

Yesterday we covered part 1, "forgetting what lies behind." Today is part two. "Reaching forward to what lies ahead...press on." You must have a goal to press toward, something to strain for or as Zig Ziglar would say, "If you aim at nothing, you will hit it every time."[5] What exactly are you straining and pressing towards? One thing should be Christlikeness which is the prize that Philippians 3:14 talks about. Some other things you could press toward are being a good mom and wife or maybe more consistent study habits and dependence on God.

Are you making choices today to be more like Christ? If so, how? If not, what is one thing you can work on? _____
_____

DAY 11

"Be anxious for nothing, but in everything by prayer and supplication with thanksgiving let your requests be made known to God. And the peace of God, which surpasses all comprehension, will guard your hearts and your minds in Christ Jesus."
Philippians 4: 6–7

I would like to focus today on the topic of being anxious or what we like to call stress. Motherhood is a unique mountain to conquer. Don't worry; everyone feels a little overwhelmed in the beginning. There are so many things to make you nervous and a large amount of debate and information on the Internet about how to raise your baby. No matter where you turn someone is telling you that you are wrong and aren't doing it right. It can be confusing. I worried about if I was feeding my baby enough, was I bad for letting her cry or allowing her sleep on her stomach. I was worried about her health issues and going to the doctors. Every visit to the doctors made me want to be anxious and worry. How on earth are we supposed to get through these stressful situations? Philippians has the answer. By prayer, supplication, and thanksgiving. These three things build on one another. You must pray and lay your burdens before the Lord. In prayer you need to ask and beg earnestly that God would help you; which is the definition of supplication. Then give thanks for what God has already given you and thank Him for what He will give you. The verse in Proverbs 17:22 "a joyful heart is good medicine, but a broken spirit dries up the bones," reminds me of the importance of giving thanks. Stress tends to narrow our focus on a particular problem, and it easily becomes overwhelming. Thankfulness broadens our outlook and lets us see the whole picture of God at work. It's like good medicine to your soul.

What are some things you are worried about? _____
_____

What are some things you are thankful for? _____
_____

DAY 12

> "Be anxious for nothing, but in everything by prayer and supplication with thanksgiving let your requests be made known to God. And the peace of God, which surpasses all comprehension, will guard your hearts and your minds in Christ Jesus."
> Philippians 4:6–7

What can you expect if you follow yesterday's lesson? Peace. Philippians 4:6 shows you what to do and verse seven gives you the results. God can take your stress and worry and can turn it around into peace, His peace. He isn't promising to take away all of your issues necessarily, but He promises an "inner calm or tranquility… [transcending] human intellect, analysis, and insight."[6] In essence, He is giving you a calm spirit in the midst of the storm of motherhood, this definitely "surpasses all understanding." When I finally started applying these verses, I was able to take my worries and questions and make confident decisions. I had plenty of worries and questions; mostly about how to take care of my baby and her health issues. I was able to make choices based on the peace of knowing that God had made me a mother and given me the tools to accomplish it. When the baby was screaming, and I didn't know what to do or how long I was going to be able to handle it I would go to the place of inner peace where God was and rest there. What makes this peace different than the world's peace? This peace helps to guard against the bombardment of stress; it is long lasting and based in an unchanging God, not circumstances. The peace of the world changes with our circumstances, God's peace remains. Your responsibility is to pray with supplication and thanksgiving.

Do you feel God's peace? YES or NO

If not, list out some of your requests then list five things you are thankful for.

Request List
1. _____
2. _____
3. _____
4. _____
5. _____

Thankful List
1. _____
2. _____
3. _____
4. _____
5. _____

DAY 13

"O Lord, You have searched me and known me! You know when I sit down and when I rise up; You understand my thought from afar. You scrutinize my path and my lying down and are intimately acquainted with all my ways."
Psalm 139:1–3

You have almost reached the two-week mark of motherhood. Congratulations! By now I am your lack of sleep is catching up to you and you probably feel like you could sleep for a week. Don't worry you are not alone. My son was born twenty-three days before my birthday, and I recall one day my husband asking what I wanted as a present that year. I told him, a full nights sleep. Ah, the wishes of a new mom. So, what does Psalms 139 tell you about sleep issues? Well, God knows what you are going through. He knows you, He knows about the day-to-day workings of your life and most importantly He knows when you lie down. Or in other words, He knows when you haven't slept and how many times you were up with the baby. Therefore He will give you strength to handle it. Did your baby stay up and cry for half the night? Don't worry, God was there, and you can call on Him for help.

Do you feel like God is with you when you are taking care of the baby? _____

_____

What are some ways you feel His presence? _____

_____

DAY 14

> "The righteous cry, and the Lord hears and delivers them out of all their troubles. The Lord is near to the brokenhearted and saves those who are crushed in spirit. Many are the afflictions of the righteous, but the Lord delivers him out of them all."
> Psalm 34:17–19

There is so much to take apart in Psalm 34:17-19 that we are going to split it into three days. We start off in verse seventeen with a great encouragement: The Lord hears you and delivers you. I think that is the cry of every woman and is an innate desire of all humans; we all desire to be heard. When we have something on our mind, we usually go to our husband or a friend because we want them to listen and make us feel better. Thankfully, God listens to you anytime night or day. He is more than just listening, He also delivers you out of all, not just some, of your troubles. Since you are focusing on being a new mom, you can cling to the fact that God hears your mom troubles. It may be that your child isn't sleeping well, you are waking up constantly during the night, people are judgmental about your choices, or your baby has health issues. God hears and will deliver you from these. How will He deliver you? Well, that's hard to say. God works in mysterious ways; it might be that He gives you strength to face it. He might take it away or give you someone to comfort you through it. No matter how He chooses to deliver you just remember that, He will. Now, unfortunately, there is a catch. The beginning of the verse talks about when "the righteous cry out." Are you righteous? Are you a believer seeking to honor God? Are you one of God's children? I challenge you to think about what it means to be righteous. God only promises this to His children and to those of His children who are living in obedience. This is not an open promise to just everyone. Evaluate our relationship to God and seek to be righteous in His sight.

Write down a few of your cries. _____
_____

What do you think it means to be righteous in God's sight? (Romans 3:21–26) _____
_____

DAY 15

"The righteous cry, and the Lord hears and delivers them out of all their troubles. The Lord is near to the brokenhearted and saves those who are crushed in spirit. Many are the afflictions of the righteous, but the Lord delivers him out of them all."
Psalm 34:17–19

Yesterday you learned an amazing truth about how God hears and delivers you out of all your troubles. That verse provides the foundation for what verse eighteen and nineteen are going to talk about. If you don't believe that God hears and will deliver you, how will you have confidence that God is near when you are brokenhearted or crushed in spirit. Before we cover verse eighteen, though, look at verse nineteen. It is important to realize as verse 19 states that "many are the afflictions of the righteous." I don't particularly jump for joy knowing that I will be afflicted. Sometimes I wrongly view my life as a Christian and think it should be all fun and comfortable. I think of my birth story (See Appendix A) and realize that it was high on the affliction scale. What are some things related to your birth that might be considered afflictions? Perhaps your doctor didn't listen or help you. Maybe you are afflicted because you can't breastfeed or that your baby doesn't want to sleep well. The first few weeks of having a baby can be full of difficulties. Maybe you are struggling with depression or anxiety. God knows you have these afflictions and again reiterates that He will deliver you from ALL of them, not just some. Take comfort in this. When Satan tries to tell you that you are alone and that no one cares you can quote these verses and work at believing what God says.

What are some of your afflictions and how can this verse help you to overcome them? _____

_____

DAY 16

> "The righteous cry, and the Lord hears and delivers them out of all their troubles. The Lord is near to the brokenhearted and saves those who are crushed in spirit. Many are the afflictions of the righteous, but the Lord delivers him out of them all."
> Psalm 34:17–19

"The Lord is near to the brokenhearted and saves those who are crushed in spirit." Just think about that for a second. Brokenhearted and crushed in spirit can bring some pretty powerful images to your mind. It is so easy for us to feel broken inside. When we feel down and depressed, we feel broken and fear we will never be put back together again. Brokenhearted means, "overcome by grief and despair."[7] Motherhood can have its moments of grief; for me, it is thinking about my labor. Six weeks after my labor it can still make me cry. I feel sadness over how it didn't go as planned. Maybe you just feel you aren't physically healing as fast as you like. It could also be something you think is small, but it is having a significant impact on you. God says He is near even if it doesn't feel like it.

Brokenhearted is easy to understand but what does it mean to be "crushed in spirit?" To be crushed means, "to suppress or overwhelm as if by pressure or weight." This reminds me of how I feel after I've had a fight with my husband. As my hormones were leveling back out, I felt a lot more on edge, which usually resulted in me fighting with my husband. Or sometimes he got mad at me for being whiny. Those arguments often left me feeling what I would consider crushed in spirit. In the context of our husbands, I want to help you realize that while you are feeling pressured by taking care of the baby and healing, your husband is also feeling a lot of pressure. He must now provide for a child. He doesn't always know how to help and feels inadequate; especially if you are constantly critiquing him when he helps. My husband hated seeing me hurting and felt overwhelmed with his extra responsibilities. Our husbands depend on us to help them feel confident in what they do, to help keep the house together and when we are recovering from birth a lot of that disappears. My husband's biggest complaint was that he wanted his wife back and the next was how long it was until we could have sex. Being a new parent takes a lot out of you and your husband. Let us not only think about how to apply this truth to ourselves but also how it might apply to our husbands.

What are some ways your husband might be feeling crushed in spirit that you could encourage him in? _____
_____

DAY 17

"Fear not, for I am with you; be not dismayed, for I am your God; I will strengthen you, Yes, I will help you, I will uphold you with My righteous right hand."
Isaiah 41:10 (NASB)

I remember some of the fears I had as a new mom: was my baby going to die of SIDS (sudden infant death syndrome)? Was she sleeping enough and getting enough food? Was my relationship with my husband ever going to seem right again? There were so many things to fear, and I had a lot of anxious thoughts. God simply states, "Fear not…be not dismayed." Why, because of Him. He is saying that He is here, He is in charge and He is YOUR God. As you learned before, He is intimately acquainted with all your ways. Look to Him in your time of fear. Don't let your fears overwhelm you.

What do you fear? _____

_____

How can trusting in God help you overcome your fears? _____

_____

DAY 18

> "Fear not, for I am with you; be not dismayed, for I am your God; I will strengthen you, Yes, I will help you, I will uphold you with My righteous right hand."
> Isaiah 41:10 (NASB)

God promises more than just being there for you. In part two of this verse, He promises strength and help. He supplies all you need whether it is help, love, a listening ear or wisdom. He upholds you. Some fears can seem crushing but God "uphold[s] you with [His] righteous right hand." These are the same hands that you cannot be snatched out of in John 10:28. This verse should bring you great comfort.

How does this help you in your struggles today? _____
_____

DAY 19

> "Seeing that His divine power has granted to us everything pertaining to life and godliness, through the true knowledge of Him who called us by His own glory and excellence."
> 2 Peter 1:3

In the last two and a half weeks, we have focused mostly on dealing with the hardships and emotions of the early days of a new baby. Now we will start to focus on moving forward in our spiritual walk. As a new mom, you tend to have only a little time to yourself, and you may feel exhausted still. Don't worry, as your child gets older, some of that will fade. In the early months, you may feel like you don't get a lot of alone time. This is why it is important to plan for a study time with God. Second Peter helps us see that even in this season, where you don't have much time, God gives you "all things" to accomplish what He wants both spiritually and physically. I think it is interesting to note that it doesn't just say "His power" but it says "His divine power." God has placed on you a special calling to be a mom, and He doesn't leave you without the resources to complete His calling. There will be days when you feel like you can't go on but remember you have the divine power of God working in you.

What do you need God's divine power to accomplish today? _____
_____

DAY 20

> "Seeing that His divine power has granted to us everything pertaining to life and godliness, through the true knowledge of Him who called us by His own glory and excellence."
> 2 Peter 1:3

Yesterday we talked about His divine power. Today, let us focus on why He has given you this power and the avenue in which He gives it. He has promised that you have been given His power for all things that pertain to life: diaper changing, sleep issues, managing a household, etcetera. Also, all things that pertain to godliness: study time, a relationship with Him and the ability to pray, just to name a few. What a relief. Some days, even the day-to-day things can seem over the top. God has given you His power to accomplish those even when you don't feel like you can. How does He make this possible? See part two of the verse, "through the true knowledge of Him who called us." So, this power is available but only in Christ and His Spirit; you only have to take advantage of it. You can take advantage of it by doing things like listening to messages online, turning on Christian music, or doing a study book. Spend time today plugging into the power of God.

Are you plugging into the power outlet of Christ? _____

How can you plan to spend more time with Christ? _____

DAY 21

> "However, let each one of you love his wife as himself,
> and let the wife see that she respects her husband."
> Ephesians 5:33

I know no one wants to hear this verse right now, but it has to be said. You can't treat your husband like crap no matter how you feel. Husbands at this time seem to fall into two categories: the ones who help and the ones who don't. Unhelpful husbands can be very frustrating for the women who are left to "do it all." This is a common complaint among women after baby number 1. You can bring this up with almost any woman and have an easy rag session on your husband; I've been there more than I'd like to admit. Complaining about your husband, I promise, is highly unfruitful. God does not negate you from obeying this verse just because you've had a baby or just because your husband doesn't help. God commands us to "respect our husband." If you want to know more on this topic, I recommend "Love and Respect" by Dr. Eggerson. As your emotions are still leveling out, it is hard to be respectful, especially if he isn't being as caring as you think he should. You are going through a tough time, and so is he. Sometimes you can simply be respectful by just holding your tongue. If you are struggling with this, I suggest writing down ten of his best qualities. Concentrating on his good qualities will help you to remember the things you love about him and not just dwell on that time he complained he was tired after you stayed up all night with the baby.

How respectful do you feel you've been to your husband on a scale of 1-10? _____

How can you improve your attitude toward him? _____

_____

DAY 22

"Let the words of my mouth and the meditation of my heart be acceptable in your sight, O Lord, my rock, and my Redeemer."
Psalm 19:14

People love to blame things on hormones. Right after birth, your hormones are swinging back and forth pretty high. Hopefully, by now they are swinging a little less. Still, they can occasionally cause to you be extremely happy then make you feel like crying the next minute, it's normal. Psalm 19:14 is a verse that can help ground you by making you focus upward. You might feel angry at your husband or worry about how well you are doing as a mom. This verse can help you to refocus on what is important to God. Ask yourself these questions.

1. Are my words acceptable to the Lord?
2. Is what I'm dwelling on acceptable to God?

Look up the following verses and explain what God wants you to think or say?
Philippians 4:8 _____

Ephesians 4:29 _____

DAY 23

> "Train up a child in the way he should go; even
> when he is old he will not depart from it."
> Proverbs 22:6

Moms tend to spend the most time with their children, at least when they are young. You get the unique privilege of helping to frame how your kid or kids will live the rest of their lives. You have a great impact on them both mentally and spiritually. Now you might wonder what that has to do with your new baby? Well, in a few short months your little one will start to develop his or her wants and desires and planning will help you (and your husband) to be ready to "train up your child." Here are a few things to ponder.

1. You can't impart spiritually to your children what you don't have yourself. If you lack self–control, don't expect your children to easily learn self-control.
2. What do you want to teach your children? Training takes purpose and a plan, or you will fail to teach them anything useful.
3. More things are caught than taught.

How well do you think you are doing spiritually for such a job? ____
_____
Write down a few things that you see are important to teach your children. _____
_____

DAY 24

> "Hear, O Israel! The Lord is our God, the Lord is one! You shall love the Lord your God with all your heart and with all your soul and with all your might. These words, which I am commanding you today, shall be on your heart. You shall teach them diligently to your sons and shall talk of them when you sit in your house and when you walk by the way and when you lie down and when you rise up"
> Deuteronomy 6:4–7

Ahh, another great passage on training your children. These verses focus on your relationship with the Lord, loving Him with your whole being and having His words on your heart. Like we talked yesterday, more things are caught than taught. As your children get older, they will watch your life to see Christ. They are more interested in what you do than what you say. For instance, if you say going to church is important, yet you don't go often you are sending them mixed messages. They will most likely conclude that it isn't important because of your actions even if you tell them it is. The same goes for your walk with the Lord. You may tell them it is important, but what do they see you do? Are you walking daily with the Lord? God says we are to teach our children diligently. When? "When you sit in your house, when you walk by the way and when you lie down and when you rise up." I think that pretty much sums up every day for the rest of your life. Each day will bring new opportunities to teach them about God.

Do you feel you are up to the challenge? _____

Where do you struggle in your walk? _____

What can you work on spiritually to be a better parent? _____

DAY 25

*"She looks well to the ways of her household
and does not eat the bread of idleness."
Proverbs 31:27*

In my generation, women talk about how they spent or will spend their first month after baby binge watching reruns. For my mom's generation, it was soap operas. I guess, truly "there is nothing new under the sun" (Ecclesiastes 1:9). There is nothing inherently wrong with watching TV, but there comes the point where it turns into idleness. When I had my first, I did spend a lot of time watching TV. I understand you are healing and tired and your brain is not functioning well enough to do much else. But there will come a time, usually after four to six weeks, when you need to get back to taking care of your household. An excellent wife takes care of her house. What exactly does that look like? Well, I would say on a basic level cleaning the bathroom, washing the dishes and doing the laundry. You may still be healing so start small and pick one or two things to clean this week. Your desire should be to please God in your household by taking care of what He has given you.

What are two things you could do this week to take care of your household? _____

_____

DAY 26

> "Not that I speak from want, for I have learned to be content in whatever circumstances I am. I know how to get along with humble means, and I know how to live in prosperity. In any and every circumstance, I have learned the secret of being filled and going hungry, both of having abundance and suffering need. I can do all things through Him who strengthens me."
> Philippians 4:11–13

Your life has changed quite a bit since your baby was born. You now have the responsibility of taking care of a new life. There will be plenty of days when you will wish you could do something else or be free of having to care for your baby all day. Contentment will help you to push on and be thankful for what you have. Whether you are a stay-at-home mom who wants to go back to work or a working mom who wants to be at home contentment is so important. God has placed you in a unique situation, accepting that and being content will help you keep going through the tough times. It is interesting that Paul says, "I have learned…" Contentment doesn't come naturally, even to the Apostle Paul. He had to learn it and so do we. He started with not basing how well his life was going on how much stuff he had but on being thankful for what he did have at the moment.

How can you work on being content today? _____
_____
Ask God to help you find the secret to contentment in all circumstances.

DAY 27

> "No temptation has overtaken you but such as is common to man; and God is faithful, who will not allow you be tempted beyond what you are able, but with the temptation, will provide the way of escape also, so that you may be able to endure it."
> 1 Corinthians 10:13

Can you think of any trials you are going through right now? You probably can. Since the word temptation can also be translated trials, it is talking about the difficulties you are facing in your life. Usually, when dealing with difficult things, we tend to feel alone and that no one could be going through what we are. God nips that lie of Satan's in the bud. He lets you know (since He sees all that is going on in the world) that your issue is common to man. You are not alone. Just the other day I was telling someone about how my son hates his car seat, and he screams the whole time he is in it. It's hard to talk to people about this because most people drive their kids around in their car seat to put them to sleep, but not mine. I felt frustrated that it was happening and depressed because no one understood. God knew this and pointed me to another mom who had the same problem. I happened to meet her in the nursery, and we shared a few horror stories, a good laugh, and now we have a common bond. Talking to her made me feel so much better, I no longer felt alone. God in His great faithfulness helped me endure this trial by sending me someone who understood what I was going through. You are probably struggling with something different but don't worry; God will provide a way for you to endure.

What trial are you or have you faced in the last few weeks or currently? _____

How has God been faithful to help you get through it? _____

_____

DAY 28

> "No temptation has overtaken you but such as is common to man; and God is faithful, who will not allow you be tempted beyond what you are able, but with the temptation, will provide the way of escape also, so that you may be able to endure it."
> 1 Corinthians 10:13

Today we are going to talk more about God's faithfulness and His love. His faithfulness and love are the two things that guarantee you aren't getting more than you can handle. Sometimes when I feel overwhelmed I think, "Wow, God must really think I'm doing well to trust me with something of this magnitude." There will be times where you feel you just can't handle it anymore. When those times come what should you do? Run and fall down at the feet of Jesus. You can also cast your cares on the Lord like we talked about a few weeks ago. He holds the escape route and it is through His power. Do you feel you won't be able to handle another minute of your baby crying or deal with another person telling you that you are doing it wrong? Well, go to God and He will provide the way for you to endure it.

What is an issue you feel you just can't handle another minute of? __
_____
How can you apply this verse to it? _____
_____

I want to congratulate you on completing this study whether it took you four weeks or eight weeks it is a wonderful thing that you desire to study God's word. Keep up the good work!

SECTION 2

CHAPTER 1

Taking a Spiritual Inventory

"Test yourselves to see if you are in the faith; examine yourselves..."
2 Corinthians 13:5a

During times of change, like having a baby, it is an excellent opportunity to take a spiritual inventory. What exactly is a spiritual inventory? Well, it's when you evaluate how well you are doing in your spiritual walk and look at areas that you may be able to improve. I suggest trying to do this before you've had your baby since, that at this point, you probably have some extra time on your hands as you anxiously wait for your baby to come. Do as it says in 2 Corinthians 13:5 "Test yourselves to see if you are in the faith; examine yourselves..."

To be completely honest, this verse in second Corinthians is not always easy to focus on. It is often overlooked in the course of one's Christian walk because taking an inventory of your life is not always fun and it can be a little time-consuming if you don't know where to start. No one enjoys having a magnifying glass look into the hidden corners of their life. Digging deep into yourself and truly being honest with where you are at is hard. Coming to grips with what you find and changing is another reason it's hard. I promise, though, it really will help you in the long run. To make it easier I have put together an evaluation for you to go through. It focuses on the main categories of your walk and how well you are doing. It should also show areas that you could use some improvement. This is just a general evaluation. There may be other areas that God will show you that is unique to you but here's a start. Be open and willing to listen to His leading. As it says in Matthew 7:7, "Ask and it will be given to you; seek and you shall find; knock, and will be opened to you (NASB)."

The Church Body

1. How important is going to church to you?
   - ☐ I go when I can.
   - ☐ I know I should go more.
   - ☐ I am usually late, but I at least tried.
   - ☐ I try to be pretty consistent.
   - ☐ It is on the top of my priority list

2. How often do you go?
   - ☐ A few times a month
   - ☐ Once a week
   - ☐ Twice a week
   - ☐ Every service

3. Are you involved in actively serving?
   - ☐ Yes, and I love it.
   - ☐ Yes, but it is just something I do.
   - ☐ Yes, but I feel burnt out sometimes.
   - ☐ No, but I'd love too.
   - ☐ No, I don't see the need.
   - ☐ No, I don't want to.

4. How committed to your church body would you say you are? Check all that apply
   - ☐ I am very involved.
   - ☐ The church body is like my second family.
   - ☐ If there are troubles, I am leaving.
   - ☐ I move from church to church.
   - ☐ I haven't found one that I like.
   - ☐ Going to church is optional.
   - ☐ People at church are hypocrites.
   - ☐ I try to work through my issues with other members.
   - ☐ I am a member of a church body.

5. Based on your answers to these questions how well do you think you are doing in the category of the "church body?" Keep in mind that Jesus loved the church to the point of dying for her (Ephesians 5:25) when thinking about how well you are doing. _____
_____

Love for Others

1. How would you rate your love for your husband on a scale of 1–10?
   1 2 3 4 5 6 7 8 9 10
   Explain: _____
   _____

2. How would you rate your love for your friends?
   1 2 3 4 5 6 7 8 9 10
   Explain: _____
   _____

3. For people that you don't like very much check how you feel toward them.
   - ❏ I ignore them.
   - ❏ I try to be courteous.
   - ❏ I only talk to them if I'm forced.
   - ❏ I pray for them.
   - ❏ I actively try and act kindly toward them.

Study and Prayer Time

1. How often do you study?
   - ❏ Daily
   - ❏ A few times a week
   - ❏ Just on Sundays
   - ❏ Every once in a while.

2. How often do you pray?
   - ❑ Daily
   - ❑ A few times a week
   - ❑ Weekly
   - ❑ Monthly
   - ❑ When I really need something.

3. How often do you confess your sins?
   - ❑ Daily
   - ❑ A few times a week
   - ❑ Weekly
   - ❑ Monthly
   - ❑ Every once in a while

4. How do you feel about your study and prayer time? _____
   _____

Recognizing Sin

1. What was the last "big" sin you confessed? _____
   _____

2. Do you feel like you sin often? _____
   _____

3. What are your top three areas of struggle?
   - ♦ _____
   - ♦ _____
   - ♦ _____

4. Can you think of a time God asked you to remove something particular from your life? _____
   _____

Dealing with Sin

1. In the last section, you answered a question about God asking you to remove something particular from your life. Did you remove it? YES or NO

2. When God asks you to remove a certain sin you most often...
   - ❏ Find a reason to justify yourself
   - ❏ Maybe God isn't really saying anything
   - ❏ You remove it for a while but end up going back to it
   - ❏ You remove it and add new good habits to keep from going back to it

3. When you do sin you most often...
   - ❏ Confess it right then
   - ❏ Confess it the next morning during your prayer time
   - ❏ Feel sad about what you did but nothing further
   - ❏ Feel sad and purpose to change
   - ❏ You seek what the Bible says about the subject and work at fixing it God's way
   - ❏ Ask for God's help to change.

4. How do you think your view of sin is different from God's? _____

Evaluation

The Church Body
- ✦ What are your strong points? _____
- ✦ Where could you use some improvement? _____

Love For Others
- What are your strong points? _____
  _____
- Where could you use some improvement? _____
  _____

Study And Prayer
- What are your strong points? _____
  _____
- Where could you use some improvement? _____
  _____

Recognizing Sin
- What are your strong points? _____
  _____
- Where could you use some improvement? _____
  _____

Dealing With Sin
- What are your strong points? _____
  _____
- Where could you use some improvement? _____
  _____

CHAPTER 2

Life Has a Way of Changing

You will find that your life is about to change in ways you never imagined. To get ready for these changes we'll cover the most common ones like your study and prayer time, your marriage, church and your home life. Let's start by looking at Ephesians 5: 15–17.

"Therefore be careful how you walk, not as unwise men but as wise, making the most of the time because the days are evil. So then do not be foolish, but understand what the will of the Lord is."

According to these verses, we are to "understand what the will of the Lord is." Thankfully, He has provided all that you need to live godly in His word; all you have to do is to ask Him to help you understand. He also touches on a few things to keep in mind while you try to figure out a new routine. You see, how you use to do things "normally" is going to be different. Adding a baby kind of mixes everything up and it takes a little bit to settle back into a new pattern. First, He says, "Therefore, be careful how you walk." You need to be purposely evaluating your relationship with Him and planning what you will do to help yourself spiritually and mentally during those first four weeks and beyond. Second, He says, "making the best use of the time." Once your baby arrives, you will feel like you have almost no time in the day. The endless feedings, naps, diaper changes and sleep deprivation make it difficult to accomplish anything. Unfortunately, we do not get a free pass from studying or praying just because we've had a baby. I am sure you wish you could get a free pass but since you don't, preparation can help you stay on track. If your priorities are not in order before your baby arrives, you will easily find your time being sucked away.

Study and Prayer

First, let's focus on your time to study and pray. Before children, my quiet time with the Lord was spent curled up in a chair with my cup of tea and my Bible. There were little if any, distractions and I could study for as long as I wanted. Waking up early to make sure I had plenty of time was not difficult at all. I kept a prayer journal and was able to quiet my mind and dwell on how I could pray for others. That significantly changed when I had my daughter. My study was less focused. I had less time and brainpower. I would read a verse and then read it again and again. Prayer usually looked like a single prayer of "please forgive me for my sins" and maybe a small prayer for help. As time progressed, my ability to study and pray got better and yours will too, as your baby gets older and you adjust to being a new mom. The first few weeks are just a little rough.

How can you deal with such a switch in your quiet time? A big part of adjusting is your perspective. For some reason, change gets a bad rap and is looked at as a bad thing when really it is just another season in your life. Looking at it as a new season will help you to embrace it instead of wishing for what you use to have. Though your time will be more limited, you will find a new fresh way to continue your relationship with Jesus. That is why it is important to "make the most of your time" like Ephesians 5:16 says. Make your time, though it is small, count for what is important. Your relationship with God is the most important thing in your life. It will benefit you tremendously during those late nights and early mornings, during the great days and the hard ones. Here are a few suggestions to help you in this time of change.

1. Talk with your husband about your desire to study. See if he can help take care of the baby so you can have maybe 15 minutes to study and pray.
2. Use the day-to-day studies in section one for an easy and practical study. They are quick and yet applicable to what you might be going through as a mother.

3. Start small with small expectations for your prayer time. Find one thing to pray for each day or develop a more "pray as you go" type attitude. I found praying during nighttime feedings was a quiet and peaceful time. This fit well with my hectic schedule until things evened out.

Remember, finding a new normal in your study schedule will take time. Here is a great verse in Jeremiah that will help to remind you that God wants you to seek Him and He promises you will find Him.

> "For I know the plans I have for you, declares the Lord, plans for welfare and not for calamity, to give you a future and a hope. Then you will call upon Me and come and pray to Me, and I will listen to you. You will seek Me and find Me when you search for Me with all your heart."
> Jeremiah 29:11–13

Marriage

Marriage is the second thing that will change quite a bit. According to Women's Health Magazine, the top problems that couples face after a baby are,

1. Your husband isn't helping enough.
2. Your husband feels like you micro-manage him.
3. You don't have sex as often as before, if at all.
4. Alone time is non-existent.
5. You clash on how to raise the kiddos.[8]

Right now we are just focusing on some of the changes that might take place in your marriage. How to solve some of these issues are in Chapter 5 How Hubby Fits In. I would love to tell you that your marriage will stay the same after a baby. Sadly, that is not entirely accurate but don't worry they are not all bad changes. Like we discussed in the study and prayer section, your outlook is critical. This is a new season in your marriage, and though it makes it harder in some ways, it also fills it with a new purpose and a deeper love. Part of what your marriage becomes is up to you.

Here are a few things that you will have to work through.

1. Time: You will have to learn to plan time to spend together. I know, that sounds so boring and structured (at least my husband did). Unless you plan you'll find your relationship will suffer. No date nights = grumpy husband. And that just won't do. There will always be things that suck away your time with your spouse. What is a day and time that you can set aside for being with each other? Ex: My husband and I would sit on the porch in the morning for about fifteen minutes and talk while the baby slept. _____

   _____

2. Household Responsibilities: Yes, that's right. You might think you can do it all. You will be the Suzie Homemaker that is portrayed in the old Good Housekeeping magazines from the 1950's. I use to pride myself on being able to conquer anything. I remember a woman at my church told me, "Just wait until you have kids, your house will never be clean." Boy, would I prove her wrong even if it killed me! I am not saying you can't have a clean house; I keep my house pretty clean even after two kids. Unfortunately, you should realize your children need YOU not always a clean house. Admit your need, especially at the beginning as you are healing. Talk to your husband about some of the ways you might need help around the house. Don't worry you can still have a clean house but you just need to ease into it.

3. Here are a few things you might need help with.
   a. Bringing up the laundry
   b. Taking the trash out

c. Washing the dishes
   d. Running to the store
   e. Doing the budget for a month or two (if that is usually your responsibility).
   f. Changing the baby's diaper when he gets home.
   g. Feeding the baby at least one to two bottles a day (if you are bottle feeding).
   h. Add a few of your own. _____
   i. _____

4. Sex: If this hasn't already changed a bit since getting pregnant it will once baby comes. Some women have an increase in their sex drive and others a decrease. Mine didn't decrease, though; it came to a screeching halt. In essence, I didn't feel like having sex EVER. This made it difficult on my poor husband. Since this is the main way wives build up and give their husbands confidence it took a ton of effort on my part to be encouraging to my husband in this way. Again, more on this in Chapter 5. I suggest having a quick discussion about when you are going to have sex again and any fears you have about it.
   What are some of your fears about starting to have sex again? _____
   _____

5. Your attitude toward your husband: You will be going through an emotional roller coaster after the baby. Parts of those emotions are an exaggerated perspective of your husband and what he does. There are days you will be angry with him for no apparent reason, then so "in love" you can't believe it. There might be days that you are paranoid and feel he is out to get you. You will need to learn to evaluate these feelings and attitudes based on facts because emotions can be deceiving. The fact is…you are hormonal remember that. Also, remember that God commands you to respect your

husband regardless of how you feel (Ephesians 5:33). You can go to Chapter 3 for more help in dealing with your emotions.

You are probably wondering at this point why God would want you to have a child and put this much strain on your marriage? The Bible does not directly tell us why He allows these marriage difficulties to come but He does tell us what He thinks about having children.

> "Behold, children are a gift of the Lord, The fruit of the womb is a reward. 4 Like arrows in the hand of a warrior, So are the children of one's youth. 5 How blessed is the man whose quiver is full of them; They will not be ashamed when they speak with their enemies in the gate."
> Psalm 127:3–5

Try your best to remember that God loves children and has given them as a gift to you and your husband.

Church Life

Third, your church life will be different. If you used to have a problem getting to church before baby, expect it to get harder. If you are okay with getting to church, then you will have to get a little more diligent. If you are a consistent attender, then you are off the hook. Okay, I am joking. No matter how often you attend or how important it is to you it will be hard to get to church. It will take preparation and diligence. Getting you and the baby ready for morning worship can be very time-consuming. As a mom, if you are involved in ministry it might conflict with your new mom duties so be open to change. Each person and couple has a different approach on this topic and needs to find their balance. Completely skipping church is an unbiblical option as seen in Hebrews 10:25.

> "Not forsaking our own assembling together, as is the habit of some, but encouraging one another; and all the more as you see the day drawing near."

Here is my personal experience in this area. I have always been actively involved in ministry at church. Before my daughter, I taught Wednesday night teen girls, played lead guitar on Sunday night and helped out in various other ministries. I realized when I was about six months pregnant that it wasn't possible for me to keep up at that pace no matter how much diligence I put forth. I prayed long and hard that God would lead me to know what He wanted me to be involved in. I had to stop teaching the teens, took six weeks off of music and stopped all other projects. I did, however, pick up nursery duty. You don't have to drop all your ministries at church, but you must realize that your priorities are now different. Taking care of your baby is one of your highest priorities.

Are there any ministries you need to take a break from? _____
_____

Home Life

Our fourth area of change is your home life. What do I mean by home life? Well, what you do with your day, your responsibilities, how you spend your time and projects you are working on. We are going to preface this with a verse.

> "She looks well to the ways of her household."
> Proverbs 31:27a

A women's role is to take care of the household and the management of the children. Some other responsibilities could include cleaning, cooking, budgeting, shopping, and laundry, etc. The Proverbs talk about someone who not only does her household duties but also does them well. I suggest discussing these with your husband. Figure out what he is expecting from you in the first few weeks and months. Your home life will mainly focus on taking care of your baby. There will be times when you want to give up, or you are sick of your life being about baby 24/7. This can cause panic when you realize that you are stuck taking care of your child. Keep in mind; in a few short months the load will get easier, the baby will become more independent. Childrearing is more of a marathon than a sprint anyway. Remember this, when you want to jump back into what you use to do. The first few months will be an adjustment period, and God has the resources and strength to help you find your new normal.

"I can do all things through Him who strengthens me."
Philippians 4:13

CHAPTER 3

Managing Your Emotions

Take a minute to think about the emotions you are feeling right now. If you are pregnant, then you may feel like you are on a small roller coaster at the carnival. Up and down, a little nauseating, but your emotions are relatively controllable. Maybe you have just had your baby, and you feel like the roller coaster has tripled in size and the ups are higher and the downs lower. You are gaining momentum now, and the hills are coming faster than ever. You're happy, you're sad, it's your fault, it's your husband's fault, you are a great mom, you are a terrible mom, you love being a mom, you can't stand being a mom and on and on. Managing your emotions right after the baby is challenging because they are on overdrive. If you keep in mind that your emotions are exaggerated, you will be able to manage them a little better.

What exactly causes this emotional roller coaster? Besides the typical hormone drop, there are a few other contributors to your emotional state. First, it's a little thing called sleep deprivation. Waking up every two and a half to three hours to feed your baby makes you slightly crazy (slightly might be an understatement). Second, it can be overwhelming taking care of all your new responsibilities. You just had a baby. I remember leaving the hospital and thinking with a mix of fear and shock that they were letting us take this baby home! Everything is new, and the responsibility of caring for a human being can be a bit much until you get the hang of it. Third, there is the whole breastfeeding thing. It would be wonderful if breastfeeding were easy. The classes make it sound like "well, you just latch the baby on and start feeding" like you are screwing on a hose to a water faucet. It is more like sticking a suction cup to your boob and having it suck out the inside. Okay, that was just my bad experience, and breastfeeding didn't go well for me. I was told that I had a hard letdown, which made breastfeeding very painful. I ended up balling my eyes out for two weeks before I quit with my first and I quit with my second day three. I admire those women who get through the first few tough weeks of breastfeeding. On the flip side, don't beat yourself up if you wanted to breastfeed and couldn't or if you are breastfeeding and people are giving you a hard time. Do what is best for you and your baby. Find people who will support you in your choices, especially when it comes to breastfeeding and bottle-feeding. There will always be someone who thinks you are doing it wrong no matter what you choose.

A Practical Guide to Managing Emotions

1. **Evaluate what you feel before you act on it.** 2 Corinthians 10:5b "Taking every thought captive to the obedience of Christ." Your emotions will be exaggerating almost everything. Don't let them run wild especially your negative emotions, stop and take a moment to analyze them. This may be hard since you are pretty tired. Your brain may not be functioning well, but it will help you not get angry at the people who are trying their best to help; mostly your husband. What emotions are you feeling? Anger? Sadness? Frustration? _____

    _____
    Are these emotions directed toward someone in particular or mostly toward yourself? Or are your emotions directed at something like the house being messy or how much sleep you are missing? _____

    _____

2. **Once you have evaluated what you feel now ask yourself "are these feelings correct?"** Philippians 4:8 "Finally brethren, whatever is true…." Is your husband really doing *nothing*, I mean absolutely *nothing*? No, he is probably just not doing what you want the way you want it; which is completely different. I suggest answering the following questions and

then talking to either your husband or a good friend about your concerns.

Are your feelings true? YES or NO

What is true about your feelings and what may be false? ___

---

3. **Remember you have the power in Christ to work through this.** 2 Peter 1:3 "Seeing that His divine power has granted to us everything pertaining to life and godliness, through the true knowledge of Him who called us to His own glory and excellence" Elizabeth George in her book *Loving God With All Your Mind*, gives some great advice about working through emotions. It is about taking one day at a time. Sometimes we have to take just one hour at a time on the tough days or even five minutes at a time. She stresses that we don't have "to handle our entire life all at once." God doesn't expect us to bear that burden, just the burdens of today.[9]

Do you believe that God has given you the power to overcome this season of emotional ups and downs? _____

There will be times when your emotions get the best of you. Don't worry it happens to all of us. Ask for forgiveness and work at thinking about what is real and true the next time. Seek out a friend who you can talk to. Others have gone through this and can help you not feel alone or depressed.

CHAPTER 4

Healing From Your Birth

If you just had your baby, you are probably wondering what just happened to your body. It is pretty amazing that a hole the size of a quarter opened up to about the size of a large grapefruit and then a baby came out. Ouch! If you had a C-section, you just had major surgery, which also is a crazy way to have a baby come out. Double Ouch! According to a study done at the University of Michigan, "Childbirth is arguably the most traumatic event the human body can undergo."[10] You may have just survived the most traumatic thing you will ever face. You may have some trauma to work through, and if you feel you might I suggest reading Appendix A. Otherwise, you will still have some healing to go through no matter what.

No matter what kind of birth you had, you will have to go through a healing process which usually lasts four-to-six weeks. Here are a few things that will help you along. This is by no means is an exhaustive list just a few pointers on the basics.

1. **Give yourself a break.** Don't push it. You might want to get back to normal as soon as possible but wait. You've just had a baby, remember, there is going to be a time of adjustment. You usually don't have to start cleaning, working out, or cooking meals right away, take a break. Take time to care for your baby the first few weeks; that alone is a full-time job. What are a few things that you feel pressured to get done? _____

   What are some of those pressing things you can put off until later? _____
   _____

2. **Avoid excessive movement.** Start off slow. The more you move and do things the longer you will bleed. Look at it this way, if you take it easy in the first two to three weeks your body will heal quicker and you will get back to full strength. The more you push it the longer your body will take to heal. I know women who bled for four to six weeks after birth because they were trying to be wonder woman and do everything they use to. If you have friends or family around, this would be the time to ask for help. Even if you take a break for a few days, the cleaning can wait. Take it easy, give yourself a break you deserve it.

    Do you have friends or family that you could ask for help from? _____
    _____

    What could you use help with? _____
    _____

3. **Using ice packs are a great trick.** They help with vaginal soreness, cut down on swelling and promote healing, according to The Midwifery Group.[11] Bringing down the swelling will make life more comfortable. Ice packs can also be helpful if your breasts are engorged from your milk coming in.

4. **Avoid super hot showers.** I know your muscles hurt, and a hot shower sounds fabulous but go with a warm shower instead. First, because you have lost a lot of blood and that much heat will make you feel dizzy and increase your risk of passing out. Second, it will make engorgement worse by causing breast stimulation and an increased milk supply; which means big, sore boobs. This will be good if you are breastfeeding but only after your body starts regulating your

supply. If you are bottle-feeding and are trying to dry up your milk, I would stay away from hot showers until your milk is fully dried up. It's hard, but it will help in the long run.

5. **Take a bath with Epsom salts.**[12] A warm bath with Epsom salts is a great way to help muscle fatigue. It can be very relaxing for your muscles and help with your frazzled nerves. See if someone can watch the baby for a half hour so you can take a nice, relaxing bath.

6. **Sleep when you can.** Yes, I know the dishes might be piling up, but this is part of giving yourself a break. Rest as much as possible in the first week. It will help calm down your emotions and also give you strength and patience to take care of your baby better. The best thing you can do is "sleep when your baby is sleeping," as the University of Michigan Hospital recommends.[13] I know most people tend to laugh at the idea but in the first week sleep at much as possible.

7. **Eat well-rounded meals.** Don't try to think about losing weight right now. Eat often so that you don't feel weak from lack of food or low blood sugar. See if you can have a few people make meals for you or come over and cook. Eating regularly also helps fight the fatigue you are feeling.[14]

CHAPTER 5

How Hubby Fits In

Involved Dad Verses Less-involved Dad

If you haven't already had a conversation about how involved husband is, you most likely will soon. Some dads are very helpful and others not so much. It is easy to complain about what men don't do or how incompetent we think they are at taking care of the baby. The attitude that you know better because you are a mom can be detrimental to you in the long run. We need our husbands whether they help a little or a lot. You are in this together, and you definitely need him, keep that in mind.

In general, there are two types of dads: the involved dad who is all in and he loves to help with whatever he can. There is also the less-involved dad that takes a more hands-off approach. Let us look at how we can help both types of fathers.

I see working with either of these kinds of dads is relatively the same. Your goal should be to "stir them up to love and good deeds" as it talks about in Hebrews 10:24. How exactly do you do that?

1. Be verbally thankful for what he does even if it is small or you expect him to do it.
2. Don't micromanage him. If he happens to put the diaper on backward, then he put it on backward. Hold your tongue and thank him for helping instead of criticizing.
3. Let him know that you need his help and that you can't do it on your own. Wait until you are calm and not frustrated, don't yell at him about what he is doing wrong. Gently express that you need his help in the most positive way possible. (Say it like you did when you were dating and asked for something. Puppy dog eyes would help too.) This is new

territory for him, and you can assume he is probably unsure about what to do or how to take care of the baby. Give him the benefit of the doubt.
4. Be specific in what you need him to do. Usually, we tend to say things like "you never help," and a man's response is usually "you never asked me to do anything." Be direct, "Can you please go change the babies diaper?"
5. Let him know that you need a break before you have a complete meltdown. Remember that meltdown help tends to be short lived. He will usually help until you stop crying and then slowly stop. If you ask ahead of time, he might see it as more long term and part of his overall responsibilities.
6. Be respectful no matter what. Ephesians 5:33 says that men are supposed to love us, and we are to respect them. Don't expect him to love you unconditionally if you don't respect him unconditionally.
7. Pray for your husband.

A Sex Break

We live in a sex filled culture. There are so many temptations out there, and as wives, we need to be aware of our husband's struggle. Men are visual, to what extent depends on the guy. Either way, we must desire to protect them from potentially sinning in the sexual category during our postpartum healing period. The scripture hits on this point in first Corinthians.

> "But because of immoralities, each man is to have his own wife, and each woman is to have her own husband. The husband must fulfill his duty to his wife, and likewise, also the wife to her husband. The wife does not have authority over her own body, but the husband does, and likewise also the husband does not have authority over his own body, but the wife does. Stop depriving one another, except by agreement for a time, so that you may

devote yourselves to prayer, and come together again so that Satan will not tempt you because of your lack of self-control."
1 Corinthians 7:2–5

Paul states that you are not to deprive one another except by agreement. It is important to talk to your husband about sex so that he knows your thoughts about it and how long you expect to wait before having sex after the baby. For instance, after my first pregnancy, we had sex four weeks after I had the baby. We hadn't discussed what was going to go on or how long we would wait. I felt we jumped into it too fast and he felt we waited too long. I know women who have waited weeks and months where others waited less than a week. It depends on your level of healing and when you feel ready. Before I had my second, we discussed that I desired to wait the full six weeks to heal. I had difficult births, and the healing process was slow. Either way, I was able to give him a time frame and discuss ways I could show him love aside from lovemaking. The best thing you can do for your husband is to communicate, even if it is about not feeling completely healed up or comfortable about sex. You need to be in agreement about when to start having sex after the baby just as first Corinthians talks about. Your husband should not have to beg you for sex, and you give him the cold shoulder instead of telling him your concerns. I had quite a few reserves about having sex again after my second. Since I communicated with my husband, he was very accommodating because he knew that I cared for him but that I was still healing.

What are a few things you can communicate to your husband about your ideas for having sex after baby? _____

If you have already had the baby, what can you communicate to your husband about how you feel about having sex again? _____

Seeing It From His Side

In chapter 2 we listed a few of the top problems, according to Women's Health Magazine, that couples face after baby.

1. Your husband isn't helping enough.
2. Your husband feels like you micro manage him.
3. You don't have sex as often as before, if at all.
4. Alone time is non-existent.
5. You disagree on how to raise the kiddos.[15]

We already discussed most of these in the last few sections, but one that I would like you to focus on is number four; alone time is non-existent. Most likely you have just recently had your baby (or you are about to), and you will come to realize that newborns take up *a lot* of time. They are 100% dependent on you for even their basic needs. Dads know this, but they want their wife back. Before the baby, you had time to sit on the couch together, watch TV together, get bored with each other, go out to dinner and focus entirely on each other. It was just the two of you and coming from your husband's perspective he has lost a lot. You have lost your time, and he has lost his wife. How can you possibly fix this? It is not like you can magically make more time. Here are a few verses in Scripture that might help.

> "Do not merely look out for your own personal
> interests, but also for the interests of others."
> Philippians 2:4

What are some of your husband's desires or interests? Is he asking for more of your time, does he want to cuddle on the couch? If you don't know just ask. _____

_____

What small changes can you make that will help him feel like you care for how he is feeling? _____
_____

> "For this reason, a man shall leave his father and his mother, and be joined to his wife, and they shall become one flesh."
> Genesis 2:24

Who are you "one flesh" with? _____
_____
Who is your top priority after God? _____
_____
Who came first, your husband or your baby? _____
_____
How does this verse apply to caring for your husband? _____
_____

> "Therefore be careful how you walk, not as unwise men but as wise, 16 making the most of your time because the days are evil. 17 So then do not be foolish, but understand what the will of the Lord is."
> Ephesians 5:15–17

What are a few ways you can make the most of your time and care for your husband as you should?

1. _____
   _____
2. _____
   _____
3. _____
   _____

What are a few things your husband might enjoy that you have the energy to give? Even the small stuff counts: A kiss when he gets home, cuddling before bed, sitting on the couch together or a little note in his lunch like you did when you were first married.

1. _____
2. _____
3. _____

This is just a season of life that is really busy for you. Make little steps to restoring balance in your marriage. Talk to your husband and soon you will find your new normal. You could also plan a date night once you feel up to it.

CHAPTER 6

Baby Basics: Sleeping & Eating

Eating & Sleeping

When it comes to the baby basics of sleeping and eating, there are only two primary goals. The first goal is that your sweet baby learns to sleep through the night. This is every parent's dream. And the second goal is that they are being fed enough so they can sleep through the night. These are interconnected by nature; a hungry baby won't sleep well.

When your baby is first born, they will be eating every two and a half to three hours. As time goes on this should change until they are eating with you just breakfast, lunch, dinner, and a few snacks around the time they reach eight to ten months old. It is often quite confusing to know when and how you should help them achieve that. The book, *On Becoming Baby Wise: Giving Your Baby The Gift of Nighttime Sleep*, "is an excellent source for getting your baby on a schedule. I will explain to you the general overview of how their plan works.[16]

Since eating and sleeping go hand in hand, we will cover the basics of both. You will find that since all babies are not created equal, you will have to figure out the schedule that works best for you. It is more of a game of give and take to find what works for you. As a mom, you have other responsibilities, so a schedule is key. There are three parts of this schedule: eating time, awake time and sleep time. To accommodate the different temperaments of kids the sections are broken down to show a range of weeks when your child may graduate to the next phase. Remember, when creating a schedule you should not be rigid. Babies are human just like us. Although we might eat lunch at eleven am most days there are times we get hungry earlier. Your baby will feel the same way. A structure will help you to avoid overfeeding your baby and causing stomachaches or not allow your baby to sleep enough causing fussiness.

Week 1-2

In the first week or two, your baby should be eating every two and a half to three hours and be awake for about forty-five minutes. That means your baby should be eating about eight times in a twenty-four hour period. If you decide to have your baby's first feeding at 8 am, your feeding times would like this, and you would put your baby to bed forty-five minutes after they wake up. They should then sleep until their next feeding or close to it.

Feeding Schedule

Feeding 1: 8 am
Feeding 2: 11 am
Feeding 3: 2 pm
Feeding 4: 5 pm
Feeding 5: 8 pm
Feeding 6: 11 pm
Feeding 7: 2 am
Feeding 8: 5 am
Feeding 1: 8 am (Cycle Starts Over)

Sleep Schedule

Nap Time 1: 8:45 am
Nap Time 2: 11:45 am
Nap Time 3: 2:45 pm
Nap Time 4: 5:45 pm
Nap Time 5: 8:45 pm
Nap Time 6: Put straight to bed after feeding
Nap Time 7: Put straight to bed after feeding
Nap Time 8: Put straight to bed after feeding

As you can see, this is where some flexibility comes in. If your baby eats at two and a half hours instead of three the exact times will no longer work. Consider this a guide. The way I did it, was to write down the last feeding time on a white board in my kitchen, or you can also just use a piece of paper. This helped me to remember when the last feeding time was even if the baby woke up from her nap early.

Another thing to focus on is keeping your baby up for forty-five minutes before putting them back to bed. At night you will want to put your baby directly to bed after feedings instead of keeping them up. What you are doing is training them to know the difference between daytime and nighttime. During your night feedings try your best to stay as quiet as possible, keep the lights dim or off and put your baby straight to bed when they are done eating. This is the beginning stage of teaching them to sleep through the night.

Week 1-2 Overview

Feedings Per Day: 8 every 2 ½-3 hours
Awake Time: 45 min
Nighttime Sleep: 3 hours

Week 3-5

Somewhere between weeks three and five, you should see an increase in the hours your baby sleeps at night. They should go from three hours a night to anywhere between four-to-six. They will start completely skipping one of their night feedings or start sleeping longer and therefore moving the time they eat to later. Here is a makeshift schedule.

Feeding Schedule

Feeding 1: 8 am
Feeding 2: 11 am

Feeding 3: 2 pm
Feeding 4: 5 pm
Feeding 5: 8 pm
Feeding 6: 11 pm
Feeding 7: 5 am
Feeding 1: 8 am (Cycle Starts Over)

Week 3-5 Overview

Feedings Per Day: 7 every 2 ½-3 hours
Awake Time: 45 min
Nighttime Sleep: 4–6 hours

Every few weeks your baby will shift in the schedule as they start sleeping longer at night. Here are two more changes that will take place.

Week 7-11

Feedings Per Day: 6 every 2 ½ hours
Awake Time: 1 hour
Nighttime Sleep: 8 hours

Week 12-15

Feedings Per Day: 5 every 3 hours
Awake Time: 1–1 ½ hours
Nighttime Sleep: 10-12 hours

This is only the first fifteen weeks, and if you want to know more, I suggest buying *On Becoming Baby Wise: Giving Your Baby The Gift of Nighttime Sleep*. Let us now take a look specifically at eating time. If you are breastfeeding, just follow the directions for the number of feedings per day. Baby should be feeding on each breast at every feeding. If you are using formula, there is a simple calculation to use in determining how much your baby should be eating at any given time.

Baby weight x 2.5 oz = # of oz baby should eat all day
Then divide that by the number of feedings per day.

Example:

If your baby weighs 8 lbs
8 lbs x 2.5 oz = 20 oz
20 oz/8 feedings = 2 ½ oz every 3 hrs (Week 1-2)

As your baby grows in weight, continue to use this calculation to make sure you are feeding baby enough food. This formula is great because it accounts for any size baby and continues to work as your baby grows. My son weighed ten pounds four ounces when he was born. He was not the normal size newborn and was eating three ounces right after birth. Without this formula, I would not have been feeding him enough because a normal five to eight-pound newborn eats about two ounces. It is just a simple way to know if you are feeding your baby enough.

Sleep Training

Often sleep training gets confused with putting the baby on a schedule. However, it is not just about a schedule but about teaching them to go to bed on their own. Think of it as a subsection of schedules. Why is sleep training important? As much as we want to cuddle and rock our little angels to sleep in the first few weeks, there will come the point when you won't want to or be able to do it. If you make rocking them to sleep a habit, it will be hard for them to fall sleep on their own. The Bible says in Proverbs, "Train up a child in the way he should go and when he is old he will not depart from it." Our job as parents is to train our children, and this is not limited to spiritual things only.

We must train them to have good sleep habits, and this will result in happy, well-rested children.

How do you sleep train? You start with teaching baby how to sleep in their crib or bassinet. When it is naptime lay them down. If you hold them all the time, they will become accustomed to being held. Follow the schedule, and you will know when they need to go back to sleep. If they get too tired, they will have a harder time falling asleep without help. At first, they will cry and cry. Go in every fifteen minutes and calm them down. Either you can pick them up or just pat their back. Once they are calm, put them back down. Eventually, they will learn to fall asleep on their own. This usually takes about two weeks of training. I will not sugar coat it, it isn't easy teaching them to fall asleep on their own, but it is worth the work. The book *On Becoming Baby Wise* has a chapter on it, but I would balance their "cry it out method" with *Secrets of the Baby Whisperer* by Tracy Hogg. She has some beneficial ideas to help your baby learn to fall asleep. Some kids will jump right on the program, like my daughter. She knows when it is time for sleep and goes to bed. She sleeps about 11 ½ hours a night. My son, on the other hand, will sleep alright during the day but at night if I can get 8 hours out of him, I consider it a good night. He is currently four months old and still waking up at least once in the wee hours of the morning. It has been a lot harder to find a schedule that fits him, and it has taken more hours to train him to fall back asleep. Remember each baby is unique, and some may take more time than others to establish healthy sleep patterns so don't give up.

CHAPTER 7

Long-Term Spiritual Fruitfulness

As a new mom, you are probably just trying to get through the day and not much more than that. Spiritual fruitfulness is probably not on that list. Having a baby is hard work. Thoughts of the future and what you want to do tends not to be something you think about at this point unless it is in the context of when you might be able to sleep again. I promise you; this too shall pass. I remember repeating this to myself over and over again as time went on. My son is five months old, and sometimes I still tell myself that. But let's fast-forward a few weeks or maybe a few months when you are starting to get the hang of things. What now?

Keep Studying

The single most important aspect of continuing to be spiritually fruitful is to study and pray daily. Find a book with a study guide or a workbook. It will help you on those days when you have a small amount of brainpower. It is necessary to set aside a time for God.

Go to Church

Going to church seems a bit obvious, I know. But getting that baby ready and making your way out the door for church can be problematic. There is so much the baby might need while you are gone and if you stick to a scheduled nap time, it is bound to be right in the middle of it. Sunday is one of the hardest days of the week for me trying to get my two little ones out the door. You will find the fellowship encouraging and also the time to focus on the Lord. Which then leads us to the next idea.

Nursery

Put your kids in the nursery. I know this seems to be a debated topic for some, but I am a strong advocate of the nursery. Why? Well, when my baby is in service with me I am distracted and learn half of what I would if the baby was in the nursery.

Second, people love watching your baby. Think of it as a way to encourage and serve others. Sometimes this is their only opportunity to hold a baby. I usually put my kids in between two and six weeks. I remember countless people telling me that they either had no grandchildren or weren't close with their kids and they loved cuddling with my children. So give them the opportunity, and they will love you for it.

Third, you get a little alone time. You may choose to wait two weeks, a month or six months before putting your baby in the nursery but I suggest doing it. If you put the baby in during the first month or two you will most likely feel some separation anxiety, it's normal. Remember you spend all day and night with them, and it is hard to let someone who is less qualified than you take care them. Give it a chance, and you will get used to it.

Listen to Audio Sermons

There will be plenty of days when you just don't have time to read and study but don't let that stop you. There are tons of apps where you can hear sermons. You can listen while you are feeding the baby or making dinner and you can start and stop them as needed. Personally, they have been a lifesaver for those days I didn't have the quiet time to study.

Continuing to be spiritually fruitful, as a mom, takes work. There are so many distractions out there and things that you need to do. Make God your first priority; it is worth it in the end.

> "But seek first His kingdom and His righteousness,
> and all these things will be added to you."
> Matthew 6:33

APPENDIX A

Healing from a Traumatic Birth

When thinking of your birth experience what comes to mind? A spiritual moment of awe and wonder or something you don't want to relive or think about? If you feel you might have suffered some trauma, even just a little keep reading.

What exactly is birth trauma? Trauma, according to the Merriam–Webster's dictionary is "a very difficult or unpleasant experience that causes someone to have mental or emotional problems usually for a long time. Medical: a serious injury to a person's body." For some of you this resonates with you, this describes what you've have been dealing with since the birth of your baby. This is how I felt after the birth of both my kids, especially my son. Are you wondering if you suffered from birth trauma? Ask yourself these questions.

- Do you feel like your life or your baby's life was threatened?
- Did you come to a point where you were fearful of what might happen to you?
- Did you feel helpless?
- Do you keep playing your labor and birth over and over in your head wondering what you could have done differently?
- How about feeling anxiety when you think about what happened or the thought of returning to the doctors?
- Do you avoid talking about your birth or avoid anything you associate with it?

If you answered yes to even a few of these you might be suffering from Post Traumatic Stress Disorder (PTSD), according to the Birth Trauma Association.[17] Yes, this is a real thing for women post labor, and unfortunately, there are not many resources about it. I'll start with sharing my story and then the things I used to work through my own birth trauma. I sincerely hope it gives you some comfort and hope. You are not alone in this.

Here is my story.

As I started writing this section, I got this feeling of tightness in my chest. My heart was starting to pound slightly, and I wondered if I actually need to share my story and if I need to relive my trauma to help you. I am on a journey of healing just like you, and I have not fully arrived yet. I still want to in some ways ignore what happened to me during labor. You see, you can't heal this type of birth trauma in a few hours of crying, it doesn't go away with the calming of your hormones or a chitchat with your girlfriend. It is something that you must deal with slowly and in levels. Our first response as Christians should be to run to Chris, first and foremost. In Christ, I found healing was faster since I came to the One who is the Comforter, Jesus Christ my Lord.

> "Blessed be the God and Father of our Lord Jesus Christ,
> the Father of mercies and God of all comfort,"
> 2 Corinthians 1:3

My story starts off on a warm summer day around nine at night. I remember like it was yesterday. I started getting my first big contractions. I was so excited. I had planned a water birth at home; I wanted a natural birth in the quietness of my own home. Some people found the idea scary since there is no medical intervention and no doctors and they would ask, "what if something went wrong." But I wasn't scared. What they didn't realize was that there was something even scarier to me than being at home and that was going to the hospital. When I was in my early 20's, I had an ovarian cyst explode, and I had a very traumatic hospital experience. The doctors were rough with me and uncaring. This caused me to start fearing doctors. That is one of the reasons I choose an all–natural birth. I didn't want to see a doctor if I didn't have too. Consider this some unresolved issues in my past. I felt by having a home birth I could avoid reliving any of these old memories.

So, when labor did finally start that Wednesday, I remember the pure excitement that I felt knowing I was going to have a baby and to top it off with no doctors. Yay! I figured in a few hours I would have my precious baby girl in my arms. I had this whole thing planned for weeks. I didn't realize you couldn't plan labor (newbie mistake). My body had other plans. Two days later my water broke, all the while I had been having contractions about ten minutes apart for a full 48 hours. I was tired but optimistic. Twenty-four hours later my contractions had stopped completely. At this point, my midwives were over my house, and they found meconium in my water, which meant the baby had pooped in the womb. That was not good. Aside from that, I had tested positive for Strep B; which is a slightly concerning infection but still manageable with a home birth. The clock was ticking, and my husband and I were left with a choice: should we go to the hospital or try to induce my labor naturally. Either way, we would be going to the hospital if the baby was not born by the next morning. We decided to go to the hospital and at two am Sunday morning I found myself at a hospital hooked up to Pitocin. If you are not familiar with Pitocin, it is the drug they use to induce labor. I tried my best to work through the contractions on my own, and I refused any form of pain meds at the beginning. I knew I could do this. In the end, I ordered morphine and after countless hours of labor had a baby girl at twelve thirty pm on Sunday. To the average person it probably doesn't seem traumatic, but with my hospital history it brought on some strong anxiety. My favorite comment was, "at least you had a healthy baby, that is what really matters." But is a healthy baby all that matters? Besides, the fact is, I didn't have a healthy baby. My daughter was born with a heart defect called Mitral Valve Regurgitation and an Ectopic Kidney.

 I was filled with regret about my birth, to say the least. To the average person, your birth story or the parts you chose to share may not seem traumatic, but you are the one who went through it. I struggled with what I went through but the people I talked to just brushed it off as regular labor issues. Regardless, I was so disappointed in myself.

I was afraid of being in the hospital even though it hadn't turned out as bad as I had expected. I think about four to five months later I was nearly healed from what I had experienced. There was a little fear but not too much. I was optimistic that my next child it would be easier.

Four months later, I was pregnant with my second. I decided after talking with my husband that I would try an OBGYN. Yeah, I know...scary. I choose this route because my fear of doctors was less than the fear that my next baby would be born with the same heart and kidney issues. Overall it was a relatively healthy pregnancy until about thirty-five weeks. My baby measured one to two weeks ahead most of my pregnancy, but it wasn't a big deal until then. I got a gestational ultrasound at thirty-six weeks, and he was in the 99 percentile for his size, which means he was already really big. That week I was in the hospital twice because I was sure I was in labor. After they had sent me home, I was disappointed and quite embarrassed because I had already had a baby and should have known it was false labor. A few days later, I woke up and was unable to get out of bed and moving around hurt so bad. I had a one-year-old to take care of at the time, and I didn't know what to do. My doctor told me to take 1000 mg of Tylenol every six hours (that was the max dose). I won't bore you with the long-term side effects of taking that much Tylenol. Anyway, I tried finding other methods to manage my pain. My doctor responded to my cry for help with my pain by telling me she was "sorry that I felt that way" which made what I was going through worse. I begged her to give me an induction because I didn't think I would be able to labor in such a state but she wouldn't budge. Finally, at thirty-nine and a half weeks, she put me on the induction list, thank God. The hospital was packed that weekend, and I had to wait three days before I was allowed to come in. I guess the pain wasn't bad enough, so I also got a lesson in patience. My husband wasn't happy about the idea of me forcing my body into labor, and neither was I. After making my way to the hospital after three days of waiting, I tried my best to hold off on the pain meds and labor naturally but for anyone who has been induced you know that is really tough. I also had a wicked nurse who decided to crank my Pitocin up every half hour until I was in so much pain I almost passed out. The nurse is supposed to monitor contractions, so they don't get too painful or long, let's just say she failed at her job miserably. My first thought was that I must have just been too tired to handle the contractions, but later my doula said that the nurse commented that she was "going to find my magic number." Pretty much she was forcing the baby out of me. I opted for morphine again. I was in so much pain; I remember hoping that I would pass out to get a moment of peace. I felt like a three–year–old, and I wanted my mommy. As I hugged my midwife, I prayed for it to end. I couldn't get out of bed to use the bathroom without passing out (because we tried it) so I was forced to pee on myself, and I was so humiliated. I wanted to die. A few hours later, I pushed out a big ten-pound four-ounce baby boy. Oh, and I got a three-inch episiotomy in the process. For someone who wanted a natural birth, I had two that were so far from it. It was traumatic not matter what anyone says and there was nothing I could do about it.

Your story is probably different than mine, or you might be reading this out of curiosity to see what some women go through. Your story matters whether it was great or small. So what are you supposed to do now? How are you expected to heal and move on?

I suggest taking a look at what the Scriptures have to say about birth and healing. God's word is a great source of encouragement for anyone going through trials, and that includes birth. Aside from that, we will also go through some practical steps that will help you deal with the feelings and memories that are locked inside.

As homework I want you to look up the following verses and answer the questions. This may take you a few days or a few weeks. Remember this is a process. Your healing may not be instantaneous or quick. Months after the birth of my son I am still working through it. Don't be hard on yourself. I suggest finding a place to study these where you feel free to be open about your emotions. I like being alone so I can cry if I want to.

How is childbirth talked about in scripture?
- Genesis 3:16 _____
- Psalm 48:6 _____
- Romans 8:22 _____

Where can you find help with your pain?
- 1 Corinthians 12:26 _____
- 1 Corinthians 10:13 _____

Who do you turn to for comfort?
- 2 Chronicles 20:9 _____
- Proverbs 3:21–26 _____
- Psalm 94:19 _____
- Psalm 56:8 _____
- Psalm 36:5–6 _____

When will you be fully healed?
- Revelation 21:4 _____
- Jeremiah 29:11–13 _____

Who knows what you went through?
- Proverbs 16:9 _____
- Psalm 34:17–19 _____
- Psalm 139:1–3 _____

How can you apply these verses in a practical way?
- Isaiah 40:31 _____
- John 14:27 _____
- Psalm 119:92 _____
- Isaiah 41:10 _____
- Psalm 33: 20–22 _____
- Psalm 119:165 _____
- Psalm 27:13–14 _____
- Psalm 25:17–18 _____

Now that you have studied what the Scripture says I want to give you some other practical advice as well. These were very helpful to me in processing what happened and what was bothering me. Again, go somewhere you can cry freely and allow all the pent up emotions to escape.

1. Write out your birth story. Write out every detail, everything you can think of, what you felt even the ugly parts you might not ever want to tell a living human being. Take your time with this. You may feel reluctant or embarrassed. Release it, let it out, cry about it and don't let it trap you. You may have to do this a few times to face what happened and start being able to see the good. I wrote mine out about three times before I got honest about what happened.[18]
2. Write out your regrets and your fears. You may have to dig deeper, and you may find old hurts that contribute to your story just as I realized I had a previous fear of doctors that added to my birth trauma.[19]
3. Once you have written out your story and your regrets and fears you will be free to move on to the next step. Start looking for the good things in your story. What are some things you felt God has protected you from? Were there any people who helped you or said something nice that comforted you? My doula was a great source of comfort, and she was a shining light in my dark story.
4. You may need to find someone to talk to. Do you have a close friend or someone you trust that you can talk with? If not, you may want to look into a Christian counselor. Sometimes admitting we need help will move us to begin healing. You should not have to do this alone. [20]

God has given us "everything pertaining to life and godliness through the true knowledge of Him who called us by His own glory and goodness" (2 Peter 1:3). He provides us His Spirit, He offers us the body of Christ, He brings you friends and family, and He gives you the ability to move on and grow out of this trial. He loves you and is always available to help. God has sent you on this journey for a reason. Let it soften you instead of hardening you. Use your suffering to comfort other women who are going through the same thing.

NOTES

Preface

1   Elizabeth Stone, "Elizabeth Stone Quotes," Goodreads, 2017, https://www.goodreads.com/author/quotes/251288.Elizabeth_Stone.

A Four Week Study

2   Mack Wayne, *Homework Manual for Biblical Living Volume 1 Personal and Interpersonal Problems*. (Phillipsburg: P&R, 1979), 63.
3   Elizabeth George, *Loving God With All Your Mind* (Eugene: Harvest House, 2005), 78.
4   John MacArthur, *The MacArthur Study Bible Study Notes* (Nashville: Thomas Nelson, 2006), 779.
5   Zig Ziglar, "Zig Ziglar Quotes," BrainyQuote, 2017, https://www.brainyquote.com/quotes/quotes/z/zigziglar617761.html
6   John MacArthur, *The MacArthur Study Bible Study Notes* (Nashville: Thomas Nelson, 2006), 290.
7   Merriam-Webster, s.v. "Brokenhearted," accessed June 11, 2017, https://www.merriam-webster.com/dictionary/brokenhearted.

Chapter 2

8   Molly Triffin, "5 Ways a Baby Messes with Your Relationship," *Women's Health Magazine*, May 28, 2013, http://www.womenshealthmag.com/sex-and-love/5-ways-a-baby-messes-with-your-relationship

Chapter 3

9   Elizabeth George, *Loving God With All Your Mind* (Eugene: Harvest House, 2005), 96.

Chapter 4

10. Lauren Bailey, "Childbirth An Athletic Event? Sports Medicine Used To Diagnose Injuries Cause By Deliveries," *Michigan News University of Michigan*, December 1, 2015, U of M Regents.
11. Midwifery Group, "Your Postpartum Body," Midwifery Group, 2008, http://www.midwiferygroup.ca/downloads/after/Your%20Postpartum%20Body.pdf.
12. Midwifery Group.
13. William Blahd Jr. and David Messanger, "Problems After Delivery of Your Baby." *Michigan Medicine*, Health Wise Staff, 2010, http://www.uofmhealth.org/health-library/tp23730.
14. William Blahd Jr.

Chapter 5

15. Molly Triffin, "5 Ways a Baby Messes with Your Relationship," *Women's Health Magazine*, May 28, 2013, http://www.womenshealthmag.com/sex-and-love/5-ways-a-baby-messes-with-your-relationship

Chapter 6

16. Gary Ezzo and Robert Bucknam, *On Becoming Baby Wise: Giving Your Baby The Gift of Nighttime Sleep*, 5th ed. (Mt Pleasant: Parent-Wise Solutions, 2012), Kindle ed. Chapter 5.

Appendix A

17. The Birth Trauma Association, "What is Birth Trauma?" *Birth Trauma Association*, 2016, http://www.birthtraumaassociation.org.uk/help-support/what-is-birth-trauma.
18. Maureen Campion, *Heal Your Birth Story: Releasing The Unexpected*, (Maureen Campion, 2015), Chapter 3.
19. Maureen, Chapter 4.
20. Maureen, Chapter 5.

Printed in the United States
By Bookmasters